ZRJC

W9-DHX-614

EDGE
BOOKS™

ALL
ABOUT
DOGS

ROTTWEILERS

by Tammy Gagne

Consultant: Deborah Shibley, Secretary
American Rottweiler Club

Capstone
press

Mankato, Minnesota

Edge Books are published by Capstone Press,
151 Good Counsel Drive, P.O. Box 669, Mankato, Minnesota 56002.
www.capstonepress.com

Library of Congress Cataloging-in-Publication Data
Gagne, Tammy.
    Rottweilers / by Tammy Gagne.
    p. cm. — (Edge books. All about dogs)
    Includes bibliographical references and index.
    Summary: "Describes the history, physical features, temperament, and care
of the Rottweiler breed" — Provided by publisher.
    ISBN 978-1-4296-3367-3 (library binding)
    1. Rottweiler dog — Juvenile literature. I. Title.
SF429.R7G343 2010
636.73 — dc22   2008055923

Editorial Credits
Angie Kaelberer and Molly Kolpin, editors; Veronica Bianchini, designer;
    Marcie Spence, media researcher

Photo Credits
Alamy/Celia Mannings, 11
Capstone Press/Karon Dubke, 1, 5, 7, 20, 21, 24, 25 (both), 27 (both)
Corbis/Bettmann, 10
Dreamstime/Pixbilder, 6 (right)
iStockphoto/cynoclub, 15; graphixel, 19 (bottom); missPiggy, 13
Lynn M. Stone, 19 (top)
Mary Evans Picture Library, 9
Ron Kimball Stock/Ron Kimball, 16
Shutterstock/cynoclub, cover, 22, 23, 28, 29; DJ Kinder, 14; Stephen Coburn,
    6 (left)

Capstone Press thanks Martha Diedrich for her assistance with this book.

Table of Contents

CHAPTER 1

THE ROBUST ROTTWEILER

Rottweilers have some of the best traits found in dogs. Rotties, as they are often called, are brave, intelligent, and loyal. They are also large and very athletic.

Because rottweilers are so big and fearless, they are excellent protectors. Above all else, though, a rottweiler is a wonderful pet. Many owners say the best thing about a rottie is its huge heart.

Is the Rottweiler Right for You?

The rottweiler is one of the most loving and loyal dog breeds. But rotties need proper training because of their size and strength.

You may have heard stories about rottweilers that have bitten people or other animals. Some people think that all rottweilers are dangerous. But the entire rottweiler breed shouldn't be blamed for the acts of a small number of dogs. Owners are responsible for training and socializing their rotties. Owners who take their responsibility seriously almost always have stable, well-behaved pets.

The rottie's size and personality make it a great protector and pet.

Finding a Rottweiler

One of the best ways to find a rottweiler puppy is to contact a responsible **breeder**. Good breeders are very picky about which dogs they breed. They want to produce healthy, friendly puppies.

Choose a puppy with a personality that fits your own. A lively puppy will make a good pet for an active person. If you like to sit quietly in your spare time, a mellow puppy may be best. Keep in mind that all rotties need activity and quality time with their owners.

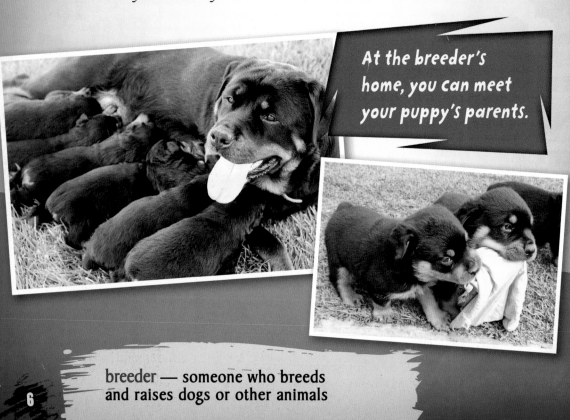

At the breeder's home, you can meet your puppy's parents.

breeder — someone who breeds and raises dogs or other animals

If you prefer an adult dog, you can find full-grown rottweilers through animal shelters and breed rescue groups. Some people think there must be something wrong with these dogs. The truth is that people give up dogs for many reasons. Some owners move to new homes that don't allow dogs. Others decide that the breed is too much work for them. To avoid this mistake, do some research before buying or adopting a rottie. Read books on the breed and talk to people who breed or own rottweilers. These sources can help you decide if the rottie is the right dog for you.

EDGE FACT

Many rottweilers serve as certified therapy dogs in hospitals, nursing homes, and schools.

CHAPTER 2

HiSTORY OF THE ROTTWEiLER

The rottweiler is named after the town of Rottweil, Germany. But most people believe the breed's ancestors came from Rome, Italy.

The rottweiler began its days as a working dog. In ancient Rome, dogs that looked a lot like rottweilers herded sheep and cattle. They also traveled with the Roman army. The dogs watched over livestock that soldiers brought along for food. This is probably how the dogs came to Germany.

Over time, these dogs developed into the rottweiler breed we know today. Germans helped with this process by **selectively breeding** the dogs.

selective breeding — the practice of carefully choosing animals to mate with each other in order to get certain qualities in their young

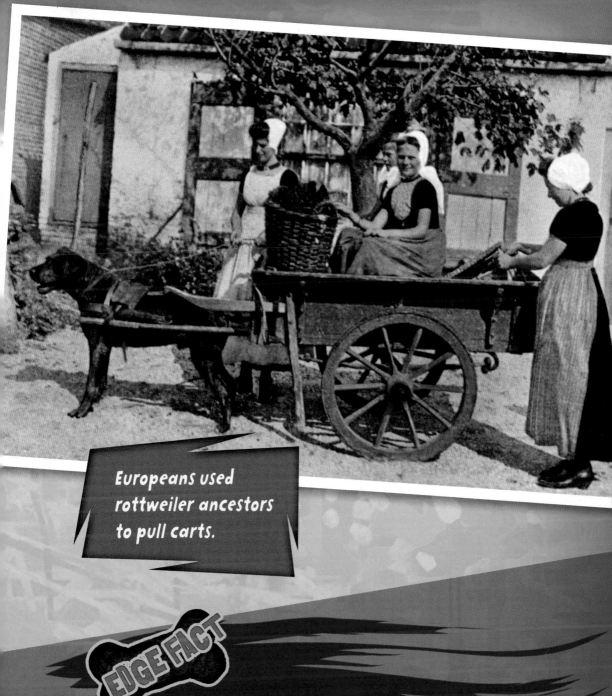

Europeans used rottweiler ancestors to pull carts.

EDGE FACT

The early rottweiler was called *Rottweil Metzger-hunt*. This means "butcher dog" in German.

Herding and Guarding

German butchers, like the Romans, used the breed for herding cattle. They also used the dogs to pull meat carts to the market. These early rottweilers held the butchers' moneybags around their necks while the butchers did business with customers.

Railroads replaced pull-style carts in the mid-1800s. But the smart rottweiler proved to be useful in other ways. During wartime, rottweilers guarded camps from sneak attacks by enemy soldiers. By the early 1900s, rottweilers also worked as police dogs in Germany.

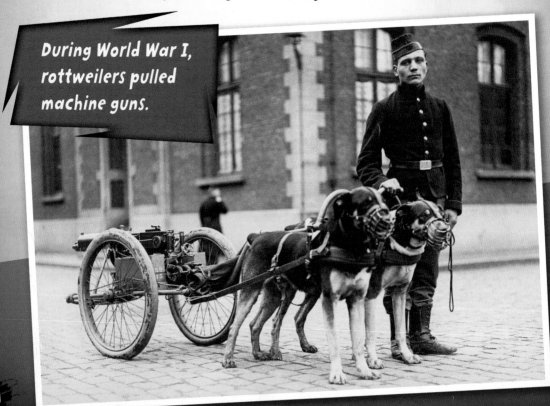

During World War I, rottweilers pulled machine guns.

American Rottweilers

German **immigrants** brought rottweilers to the United States in the 1920s. Americans began breeding rotties in the 1930s. However, the breed didn't become well known in the United States until the 1970s.

Today rottweilers are still used as working dogs. They serve as police, search-and-rescue, and guard dogs. Many other rotties are kept as pets.

Some rotties work with the police and the military.

immigrant — someone who comes from one country to live permanently in another country

CHAPTER 3

STRONG AND STURDY

The first thing people usually notice about a rottweiler is its size. Many people are also amazed by how sweet this large breed can be. Rotties truly adore their owners.

Size and Color

Male rottweilers measure between 24 and 27 inches (61 and 69 centimeters) tall. Females are smaller, usually between 22 and 25 inches (56 and 64 centimeters) tall. Dog show judges prefer dogs that are somewhere in the mid-range of these measurements.

The rottweiler's size isn't the only thing that sets it apart from other dogs. The breed's coloring is especially striking. Rotties have a black coat with rust-colored markings. Some people compare the markings to the color of mahogany. This red-brown wood is used for furniture and floors.

Rottweilers are prized for their rust-colored markings.

Body Features

Like everything else on a rottie, its head is large. The ears are shaped like triangles. They fall forward to lie flat against the face. A rottie's eyes are dark brown. Their alert, intelligent expression makes the dog look like it can handle anything that comes its way.

The rottweiler's coat is short and thick. An undercoat is beneath the hair on a rottie's neck and thighs. The undercoat helps keep rotties warm. A rottweiler's undercoat may be thin or heavy, depending on the climate.

Rotties have two coats of fur.

breed standard — the physical features of a breed that judges look for in a dog show

muzzle — an animal's mouth, nose, and jaws

Markings

The rottweiler **breed standard** says the dog's markings should appear only in certain areas. A rottie should have a spot over each eye. It should also have markings on its cheeks and the side of its **muzzle**. The forelegs, the inside of the rear legs, and part of the chest should be rust-colored as well. No markings should be on the bridge of a rottie's nose.

Dogs that don't fit the breed standard can't compete in shows, but they can make great pets. Dogs sold as pets are also less expensive than show-quality ones.

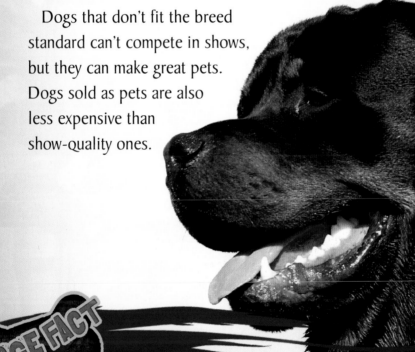

EDGE FACT

A healthy male rottweiler can weigh as much as 135 pounds (61 kilograms).

Rotties love to play games with flying discs and other toys.

Temperament

The rottweiler is not a dog that greets strangers with kisses. Most rotties need some time before they trust new people. But once a rottweiler decides it likes you, you have a friend for life.

Rottweilers are very smart. They are also eager to please their owners. This makes training fun for both owners and dogs. Owners can reward a well-behaved rottie with a treat. What these dogs like most, though, is lots of praise.

Avoid playing games that teach your rottweiler to act aggressively. Tug-of-war, for example, teaches a dog to challenge people. All types of play should encourage your dog to work with you, not against you.

EDGE FACT

When they are happy, some rottweilers make a purring sound.

CHAPTER 4

CARING FOR A ROTTWEILER

Owning any dog is a big responsibility, but caring for a rottweiler is an enormous one. These dogs need lots of attention and training. They also eat more food and need more exercise than smaller dogs do.

Training a Rottweiler

A rottweiler's training should begin at birth. Sign up for an obedience class even before you bring your rottweiler puppy home. In puppy kindergarten, your rottie will learn how to play well with other dogs and people.

Work on training your rottweiler at home as well. Otherwise, your rottie may learn bad habits like jumping on people. Bad behaviors are much easier to prevent than correct later. It is also best to train puppies when they are young because of their small size. If you wait until your rottie is big and strong, training will be much harder.

Rottweilers must also be socialized. This means safely introducing your dog to as many people and other pets as possible.

Rottie training should include both obedience and socialization.

Feeding a Rottweiler

Rottweilers need nutritious food. The most popular food choice of most dog owners is kibble. But remember that all brands of this dry dog food are not the same. The highest-quality kibble is sold at pet supply stores.

The amount of food your rottweiler should eat depends on its size, gender, age, and activity level. Eating too much food is bad for any dog. Overweight dogs are more likely to get sick. One of the best ways to keep your dog healthy is by keeping its weight within the normal range. Your veterinarian can tell you what your dog's weight should be.

Eating crunchy kibble helps keep rotties' teeth clean.

EDGE FACT

Check your dog's weight by feeling its ribs. If you need to press deeply into your rottie's rib cage to feel its ribs, your dog probably needs to lose a few pounds.

Exercising a Rottweiler

Rottweilers need daily exercise to stay fit. Walks are a good start, but they are not enough for this breed. Join in whatever activity you choose for your pet. Going on a hike or jog? Strap on the leash and bring your dog with you. Rottweilers enjoy many other fun activities too. Play ball with your rottweiler at the park or take it to the beach.

Rottweilers have fun exercising with their owners and other pets.

Agility contests test a dog's running and jumping abilities.

Rottweilers can also get exercise by competing in organized events. In agility contests, dogs run across ramps and through tunnels. Many rotties also enjoy carting events. In these contests, dogs pull loaded carts. Rottweilers often do well in carting events because of their history of pulling meat carts for butchers.

Grooming a Rottweiler

Grooming a rottweiler isn't a big job. A weekly brushing and a monthly bath should be enough to keep your rottie's short coat clean. But don't put off these important tasks. Rottweilers can shed a huge amount of hair if they aren't brushed regularly.

You will also need to clip your rottweiler's nails and brush its teeth. Nail trims can be done every few weeks, but toothbrushing should be a daily job. You can buy dog toothpaste and shampoo at a pet supply store. Products made for people can make dogs sick or dry out their skin.

Regular brushing helps prevent shedding.

Brush your rottie's teeth every day and bathe it once a month.

A Healthy Rottweiler

Your number one partner in keeping your rottweiler healthy is its veterinarian. Your rottie should visit the vet at least once a year. The vet will weigh your dog, take its temperature, and check its joints. The vet will also give your dog any necessary **vaccinations**.

Some health problems are more common in rottweilers than in other breeds. Rotties can suffer from hip or elbow dysplasia. This means that the dog's joints do not fit together properly. The condition can be painful, but surgery or physical therapy can sometimes fix it.

Another problem many rotties face is bloat. This condition causes the dog's stomach to fill with gas. Bloat can become serious and sometimes cause death. To help prevent bloat, make sure your dog rests after its meals. If your rottie's stomach looks unusually large after a meal, take the dog to your vet right away.

Also schedule an appointment to have your vet spay or neuter your rottweiler. These simple operations prevent dogs from having puppies. Having your dog spayed or neutered helps reduce the pet population. It also reduces your dog's chances of getting diseases, including some types of cancer.

vaccination — a shot of medicine that protects animals from a disease

Veterinarians help
keep rotties healthy.

A Faithful Friend

Buying or adopting a dog is easy. Being a good owner is a lot tougher. But if you train and care for your rottweiler properly, it just might be the most rewarding job you'll ever have.

Rotties give back the kindness and love they are shown.

Glossary

breeder (BREE-duhr) — someone who breeds and raises dogs or other animals

breed standard (BREED STAN-durd) — the physical features of a breed that judges look for in a dog show

dysplasia (dis-PLAY-zhah) — a condition in which an animal's elbow or hip joints do not fit together properly

immigrant (IM-uh-gruhnt) — someone who comes from one country to live permanently in another country

muzzle (MUHZ-uhl) — an animal's nose, mouth, and jaws

physical therapy (FIZ-uh-kuhl THER-uh-pee) — the treatment of diseased or injured muscles and joints with exercise, massage, and heat

selective breeding (si-LEK-tiv BREED-ing) — the practice of carefully choosing animals to mate with each other in order to get certain qualities in their young

vaccination (vak-suh-NAY-shun) — a shot of medicine that protects animals from a disease

Read More

Fiedler, Julie. *Rottweilers.* Tough Dogs. New York: PowerKids Press, 2006.

Gray, Susan Heinrichs. *Rottweilers.* Domestic Dogs. Mankato, Minn.: Child's World, 2008.

Stone, Lynn M. *Rottweilers.* Eye to Eye with Dogs. Vero Beach, Fla.: Rourke, 2005.

Internet Sites

FactHound offers a safe, fun way to find Internet sites related to this book. All of the sites on FactHound have been researched by our staff.

Here's all you do:

Visit *www.facthound.com*

FactHound will fetch the best sites for you!

Index